*Knebworth '96*
*Photo by Mick Hutson*

# KNEBWORTH

*30 years of the greatest rock venue in the world!*


*compiled. designed and edited by*

*Henry Lytton Cobbold*

*additional design by*

*Leigh Allan*

*principal photography by*

*Sim Scott*



a39bk

*My sincere thanks to :*

*Leigh Allan ~ for hours and hours of slicing photos and brilliantly breaking the blank page.*

*Chryssie and David Cobbold ~ for 30 years of building this extraordinary brand from an empty field... and for getting up very early in the morning to spread out a sleeping bag and save us a place.*

*Freddy and Wendy Bannister ~ for their help in, and support of, this project... and for that blessed day they went looking for a site for a Renaissance Fair.*

*The photographers ~ especially the wonderful Sim Scott... and Chryssie Cobbold, Patti Razey, Leigh Allan, Mick Hutson, David Brown, Nigel Barton, Richard Young, Cito Franco, Denis O'Regan, Simon Robinson... there are others, who's names are not available to me, but to whom I am even more grateful for forgiving omission... thank you for making this book possible.*

*The journalists, publications and personalities that I have quoted, especially Chryssie Cobbold ("Knebworth Rock Festivals"), Freddy Bannister ("There Must Be A Better Way") and George Pruette... you too have made this book possible.*

*And those - I'm thinking of you in particular, Ben - who, over the years, have painstakingly pasted all the clippings into books in the Knebworth Archive.*

*And especially all the bands, promoters and production companies who are part of this story and therefore who's images are to be found embedded in these pages - where possible with permission, where not, with entreaty for understanding of the spirit of the undertaking.*

*My family ~ for living with me through my deadlines.*

*And our neighbours ~ for that one weekend, occasional summers, when we make their lives difficult... I, and hundreds and hundreds of thousands of others, say thank you.*

**KNEBWORTH** *30 years of the greatest rock venue in the world!*



Published by:
The 39 Production Company Ltd.
P.O. Box 10
Knebworth
Herts SG3 6PZ
Great Britain
http://www.the39.com

Additional cover work by Dean Harmer at Aitch
Pre-press by Zoe Solley at Icon
Printed by Proost in Belgium

ISBN: 0-9539649-2-2

*This book is a collection of some of my favourite images and stories from 30 years of Knebworth Concerts.*

*Two million people share these memories. They were the summers of our youth. They were our escape from everyday worlds. They were early pilgrimages to the hillside of our heroes. They were lost moments with RonnieVan Zant(Lynyrd Skynyrd), John Bonham (Led Zeppelin), Dennis Wilson (The Beach Boys), Freddie Mercury (Queen), all of whom left this world soon after... and mass triumphal chants to "Hey Jude", "Roll With It" and "Let Me Entertain You". They were our music, our time... inFreddie's words, they were the days of our lives.*

*My kids are now the young teenagers that I was in 1974 when my parents hosted the first "Bucolic Frolic". Another generation is set to make Knebworth its own. Here's to the next 30 years... may they have such memories as these!*

*Henry Lytton Cobbold*
*Knebworth House*
*Summer 2003*

# KNEBWORTH *then & now*

## The Hon David Lytton Cobbold at home with his family

### A warm welcome to all our visitors !

Knebworth Park has in the past few years become an established family favourite. To us who have known and loved Knebworth all our lives, it is a privilege and a pleasure to see so many people young and old enjoying the beauty of its parkland and the fascination of its history.

By coming here to Knebworth you are helping us to preserve and sustain a part of Britain's heritage — **your** heritage and that of your children and grandchildren.

As a trustee of that heritage, I have a challenging occupation. Look around you—you can easily see the problems—the crumbling masonry, which needs restoring, the ageing chestnut avenues, which need replanting and of course the lawns and flower beds which need constant attention.

We aim to solve these problems but we cannot possibly succeed without your help.

I hope that you enjoy your visit to Knebworth.

Thank you for coming! Thank you for your support!

**David Lytton Cobbold**

## What's in the Park

An established favourite for an increasing number of families, Knebworth Country Park — the first privately owned Park to be sposored by the Countryside Commission—offers improved facilities and new attractions for 1976.

**Adventure Playground.** If your children haven't taken you to our Adventure Playground yet, then we suggest you give them a surprise treat without delay and don't blame us if you have to drag them away! While the kids are exploring tree houses, negotiating rope walks and tunnels, you can have a quiet picnic or sample some of Knebworth's many other attractions. If you're young at heart you may like to join the kids on the fabulous ASTROGLIDE or go for a bounce in the 90ft WHALE.

**Bird Garden.** Mike and Ann Tunnicliffe's collection of exotic birds is becoming a major attraction of the Park. Mike and Ann concentrate on letting the birds fly free and it is a common sight to see in the Park brightly coloured macaws flying in formation with a majestic pelican. In addition to its regular occupants, the bird garden is often host to lion cubs and other animals.

**Narrow Gauge Railway.** The Railway winds through the Park for over a mile, linking the Adventure Playground with the Barn Restaurant complex. The whistle of steam engines and the hiss of steam can be heard on busy days when the train is pulled by one of the historic steam quarry engines which have been restored at Knebworth. The steam engines puff their way through avenues of chestnut trees past herds of deer and old English Soay sheep.

**Deer Park.** Approximately 150 deer of three varieties—Red, Fallow and Machurian Sika—roam the Park, as deer have done at Knebworth for over 300 years.

# 1490

THE LYTTON FAMILY CLOSE ESCROW ON A FEW ACRES IN HERTFORDSHIRE ...which was possibly already owned by the in-laws. The music begins in the 1760s when widowed Leonora Lytton marries James Oswald, one of Scotland's foremost composers, who reputedly writes the melody for Robbie Burns' "Ae Fond Kiss" - one of history's earliest top tunes - and the now lesser known "Knebworth Jig".

*Edward Bulwer Lytton (1803 -1873)*

*his death mask*

# 1844

KNEBWORTH'S GOTHIC SPIRES AND GARGOLYLES DREAMT UP BY GENIUS AUTHOR EDWARD BULWER LYTTON ...whose novel "Rienzi" inspires Richard Wagner's breakthrough opera; whose play "The Lady of Lyons" inspires the first American Opera; whose novel "The Last Days of Pompeii" inspires John Philip Sousa's favourite suite (preferred even to the Monty Python theme); and whose supernatural tale "A Strange Story" inspires Elgar's Piano Quintet - but who apparently didn't have an ear for music

# 1971

CRUMBLING GOTHIC PILE OPENS ITS GATES TO THE PUBLIC IN A LAST BID ATTEMPT TO SAVE ITSELF ...but music doesn't initially feature in these plans. A giant inflatable whale does.

# 2003

KNEBWORTH HOSTS THE BIGGEST MUSIC EVENT IN BRITISH HISTORY ...and although it's still the home of the Lytton family, still a happy playground on a summer weekend, still rich in history and the heritage of Edward Bulwer Lytton and his illustrious forebears and progeny - and still falling down - Knebworth is, in 2003, best known across the world... for music.

## Welcome to Knebworth

*I hope your visit will be a special occasion for you. The Lyttons, my grandmother's family, have lived here for 500 years.*

*Queen Elizabeth I stayed at Knebworth, Charles Dickens acted in private theatricals in the House and Winston Churchill's painting of the Banqueting Hall hangs in the room where he painted it.*

*A walk through the House is a walk through history. Robert Lytton, Viceroy of India, proclaimed Queen Victoria Empress of India in 1877. Constance Lytton, militant suffragette, fought for votes for women in the early 1900s.*

*With the Park, Gardens and Adventure Playground, there is something for all the family.*

*Have a great day and thank you for sharing our home - its past, its present and its future.*

*The Hon. Henry Lytton Cobbold and his wife, Martha Lytton Cobbold*

## Opening Times 2003 (subject to special events)

*Daily:* 12 April - 27 April; 24 May - 1 June; 5 - 31 July; 4 Aug - 2 Sept incl.
*Weekends & Bank Holidays only:*
29 March - 6 April; 3 May - 18 May; 7 - 9 June; 6 - 28 Sept incl.

**Park, Gardens, Playground & Railway** 11.00am - 5.30pm
**House & Indian Raj Display** 12.00noon - 5.00pm (last admission 4.30pm)

## House Tours

All tours are guided, except on busy weekends, when "free-flow' tours operate with House Wardens in key areas. Groups will be split into parties of 25 maximum. Guided Tours take apprioximately 1 hour; however, we can vary the timing and content of a tour to suit the interests and needs of the group.

## Admission

**To House, Gardens, Park, Playground & Railway**

| | Excluding House | Including House |
|---|---|---|
| Adults | £5.50 | £7.50 |
| Senior Citizens | £5.50 | £7.00 |
| Children (4-16) | £5.50 | £7.00 |
| Family Day Ticket (4 persons) | £19.00 | £25.00 |
| Season Ticket (1 person) | £25.00 | N/A |

Pre-booked Special Interest and School Group tours are available daily from 29 March to 28 September (including Evening Tours), subject to confirmation. Please contact the Group Bookings Co-ordinator for a copy of our Groups Brochure, or to make a booking.
Admission prices may be adjusted on certain days for special events or at the Management's discretion at any time.
CHILDREN UNDER 4 ARE FREE. All prices include VAT.
**Personal Season Ticket £25**: A season ticket will allow you an unlimited number of visits during normal opening hours to the Gardens, Park and Fort Knebworth and many special events.

**Disabled Access**: Information regarding access for disabled visitors is available on request.

**Knebworth House, Knebworth Park, Hertfordshire SG3 6PY**
**Tel: 01438 812661 Fax: 01438 811908**
**Email: info@knebworthhouse.com**
**Websites: www.knebworthhouse.com**
**www.knebworthhousegiftshop.com**

# IN THE BEGINNING...

...there was Knebworth and Freddy Bannister looked out over the face of the park and said: "Let there be musi
And lo, more than 100,000 people turned up and saw that some of it was good and some of it wasn't!

*Roger Fulton Midweek Times 27 Jun*

Events.

**Frederick Bannister Promotions Ltd.**

22 Trevor Place, London, S.W.7
Telephone: 01-584 3428
Telex: (GRUNT REC. LON) 918 782
VAT No. 238 9988 85

040 377 292

5th. February,1974.

Dear Mr. Condy,

I don't know quite how to put this, but when you kindly showed my wife and I the park I was struck by the obvious suitability of the area for a one day popular music concert. I was not, I can assure you, going to take this any further, but by an amazing, and genuine coincidence I received the very next evening a phone call from the manager of a well known group expressing interest in my company promoting an outdoor event, featuring his group. I realise it is rather presumptuous of me but I wondered if you could possibly submit the following proposals to The Hon. David Lytton Cobbold:-

I. My company is interested in renting the park for a one day popular music concert aimed at attracting between 30-35,000 persons.

2. I am prepared to offer a rent of £12,500, plus V.A.T. payable, of course, in advance. In addition, I am prepared to offer a legal contract guaranteeing, amongst other things, that the site will be returned to its original condition, also, if it is considered necessary, I would be prepared to deposit a lump sum into escrow as an indemnity.

3. The concert would be scheduled between noon and 10 p.m. and sufficient transport would be arranged to return everyone home the same night.

4. Security would be in the hands of Securicor and sufficient men would be engaged to ensure maximum security of the estate.

5. Full co-operation would be maintained with the local authorities.

We said we were sorry, but the answer was no. We had been asked by promoters before about holding concerts in the park; we didn't think pop festivals were the right image for stately homes; we valued our local reputation too much and were also a trifle scared at the idea of having thousands of rock fans all over the park. We had always said no in the past. But Freddie was very persuasive. Everything had a price, he said, and asked us to name ours. We suggested a five figure sum, never dreaming he would accept... *Chryssie Lytton Cobbold*

I was, as the expression goes, totally gobsmacked. The park was just what we had been looking for to stage a one-day concert... Not only was there a gently sloping arena but there was also a huge area of flat land nearby for car parking, as an added bonus there was even an excellent road system in place that ran around the entire periphery of the park. With all thought of a renaissance fair gone I rang Peter Grant. "Have I got a site for you," I said, "Only twenty eight miles from London, a huge park, a natural arena, and access straight off a motorway."

*Freddy Bannister*

- 2 -

6. Having organised three similar outdoor events I am in a position to offer a large number of references including landlords, police forces, councils etc.

In closing, I would like to emphasise that when I originally approached you, through Monkton and Partners, my interest in running a large scale medieval entertainment was genuine and not in anyway an elaborate subterfuge.

I look forward to hearing from you.

Sincerely,

Freddy Bannister

(Frederick Bannister)

Led Zeppelin

D.C.L. Condy Esq.,
The Manager,
Knebworth House,
Knebworth,
Herts.

The following Thursday the Melody Maker carried on its front page in huge letters the headline 'Together for just one show Zeppelin, Allmans!' Joint equals. Oh my God that's it. I knew that Peter didn't consider any band to be Zeppelin's equal let alone The Allmans... The next day we received a telegram from Peter Grant thanking us for our kind offer but explaining that recording and film commitments prevented them from accepting... Do we fold the whole thing? Or should we go ahead with what was basically our support programme albeit a very strong one?... *Freddy Bannister*

# KNEBWORTH '74

## STATELY HOME IS GOING POP

A STATELY home is to open up its gates to thousands of discerning fans in a summer pop extravaganza. A one-day event of modern progressive music will take place in Knebworth Park, Herts., on Saturday July 20 and it is thought that up to 100,000 may attend. Evening News 29 May 74

THE ALLMAN BROTHERS BAND promise one of the epic rock extravaganzas of the year when they make their British debut at Knebworth Park, Hertfordshire, this Saturday. The band will be playing for a minimum of three and a half hours. And that's official. It's written in their contract with promoter Fred Bannister. The Allman Brothers - America's biggest live draw - have never before appeared outside of the United States. *Melody Maker 20 July 74.*

Unlike any of our later Knebworth Festivals we did not apply for a licence. As the event only lasted for one day we did not think it necessary. A conclusion that was disputed by the local licensing officer, Mr Pruette, who only heard about the event from his daughter who had read about it in Melody Maker. *Freddy Bannister*

Late Saturday night the pop festival was a picturesque sight. Knebworth rose floodlit out of a sea of reflecting car roofs which stretched down the hillside. Many of the fans were just standing and looking. "Isn't that gorgeous," one girl was heard to remark. "I never knew a house could look that beautiful." *N Herts Gazette 25 Jul 74*

The organisers had seen fit to provide one of the best outdoor PA systems that I've ever heard at a festival... A massive stack of speakers, which were directed through huge horns, ensured that the sound was crystal clear... Wherever one was in the audience, one got a great sound. *Dave http://tinpan.fortunecity.com/ebony/546/knebrec74.html*

All around us were parked fine cars, lovely women passed to and fro and if you lay just so, you could see their breasts through the thin material. Children called Cosmos and Tarquin played with amusing dogs, and exquisitely thin young men, carefully carefree in dress, looked at one another and wondered who scored the higher on the Far-Outometer. *John Peel Sounds 27 July 74*

Even the gloomiest of us have to admit that the Knebworth Festival was indeed pretty knice. *Chris Salewicz New Musical Express 27 July 74*

## KNEBWORTH: THE PERFECT DAY OF ROCK

To try and describe the Allman Brothers is something akin to impossible. It was like a classical music lover hearing Beethoven in person, or a teeny bopper having Rod Stewart singing in her front room. The atmosphere was one of intense pleasure and involvement with one of America's greatest bands. I can still look back on Knebworth and say it was the best concert I have ever seen. Fred Bannister you hit the Jack Pot!! *Dave Richard and Jude Riley Review July 25 1974*

# KNEBWORTH '75

## FLOYD SAY YES TO KNEBWORTH *front page headline NME 26 April 75*

I was quite surprised at the amount of opposition we faced, mainly from people who I learnt later had not even attended the concert to see for themselves what it was like. As someone with strong socialist views I couldn't believe it when a Labour Councillor got to his feet. "What I really want to know," he exclaimed, "is where the vast profits from these concerts go, is it right that they should go into one man's pocket?" Does he mean the loss I made last year I thought? The Chairwoman immediately pounced on him, "We are here to discuss the issuing of a music licence your question is totally irrelevant." We finally won by a reasonable majority but it is interesting to note that most of the young labour councillors voted against us, and virtually every one of the little old Tory ladies voted for us. Not at all what I was expecting. *Freddy Bannister*

Two girls were among 25 fans arrested for possessing drugs *The Sun 7 July 75*

David issued an invitation to the Pink Floyd band and crew to come up to the House afterwards. I wasn't prepared for them and rushed back to the house. The study seemed fairly respectable and I didn't expect many of them to turn up. I hurriedly searched around for ashtrays, glasses and some drink, but after twelve hours of music and sixteen hours of sitting on the grass in the park I wasn't feeling particularly bright. I had no idea who the Pink Floyd musicians were or what they looked like. I believe members of The Who were there too. It was impossible trying to sort out the musicians and their guests from the gate crashers. I would ask someone who they were and they would say "a ligger". I hadn't a clue what a ligger was but it seemed to be the password for entry into the House and a free drink. To make matters worse, the police and drug squad turned up looking thirsty and wanted to recap on the day's events. I found myself giving them whiskies in the hall while the group and their friends were in the study, for all I knew rolling up joints or worse. *Chryssie Lytton Cobbold*

Three North Herts councillors announced this week that they have changed their minds about pop concerts - after witnessing the placidity of audiences attending the Knebworth concert in July... "I was one of the opposition, but I must say that I have changed my mind as far as this concert is concerned. I received only one complaint and I thought the whole affair was very well organised, " Councillor Dumelow commented. *Hitchin Gazette 18 September 75*

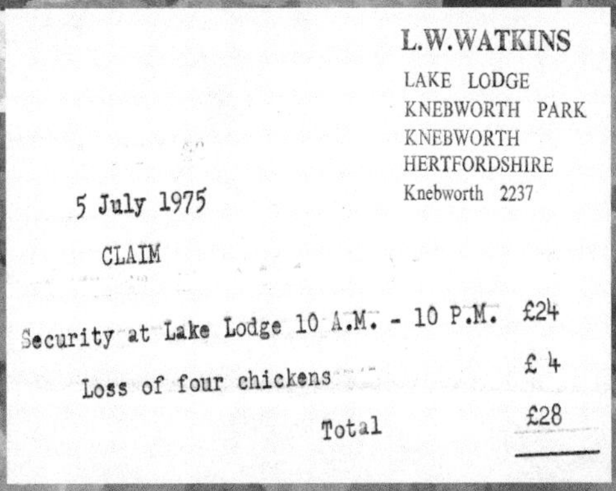

L.W.WATKINS
LAKE LODGE
KNEBWORTH PARK
KNEBWORTH
HERTFORDSHIRE
Knebworth 2237

5 July 1975

CLAIM

| | |
|---|---|
| Security at Lake Lodge 10 A.M. - 10 P.M. | £24 |
| Loss of four chickens | £ 4 |
| Total | £28 |

No one could argue that the Knebworth Festival was not the outdoor event of the year. *Disc 12 July 75*

# KNEBWORTH '76

## ROCKING SHOCK IN STORE FOR A QUIET OLD VILLAGE

They will be bringing in the horses and locking the gates this week in old Knebworth. For the denim hordes are coming. The summer stillness of the quiet Hertfordshire village - one shop, one pub and a cluster of old-world cottages - is about to be rocked by the greatest band in the world. *Mandy Bruce The Evening News 17 Aug 76*

## THIS COULD BE THE LAST TIME

The Rolling Stones play Knebworth at the weekend amid speculation that it is the last time they'll appear live in this country... "When bands have been around this long," guitarist Keith Richard is reported to have said, "they should be dead and buried." And says Jagger: "I would hate to think I would still be singing Satisfaction when I'm forty." *Maurice Chittenden Luton Evening Post 20 Aug 76*

I don't know much about this group that's coming - but they play the same kind of music, I think, as the ones last year. And that was really quite pleasant. They seemed quite a nice group of young people. *Knebworth pensioners Dennis and Violet Grimwood*

They held a sound check on the Thursday night before the concert, a hot summer evening... there was just the band on the vast stage with a dozen or so people sitting on the grass in the evening sunshine. It was magic. Not so, unfortunately, for the battleship-built Girl Guide commandant who was in charge of about 50 Guides camping at the other end of the park... she marched down to the stage, elbowed her way past all the security guards and grabbed Jagger by the arm. "Young man," she shouted, "this noise must stop. My girls can't hear themselves sing." *Chryssie Lytton Cobbold*

250,000 people in the middle of an English drought. No overdoses and nobody hurt... and that's a lot of people to put in onc place. And it was Todd Rundgren, Hot Tuna, 10cc, Clearwater Revival, the Rolling Stones and us. And we blew the Rolling Stones off the stage.

*Artimus Pyle of Lynyrd Skynyrd "Freebird The Movie" ~ not all true, but the drummer's last claim is hardest to argue.*

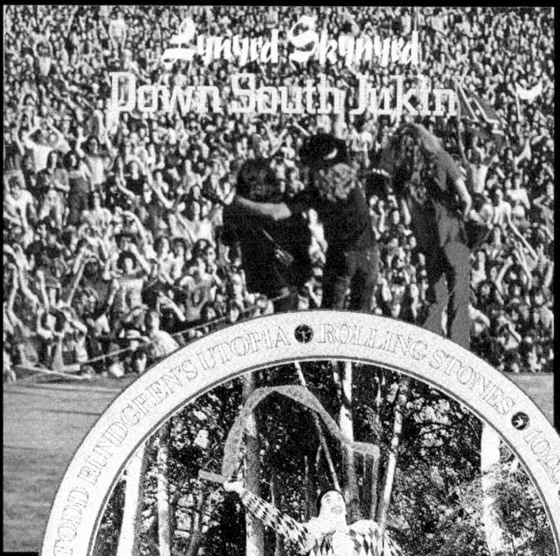

No-one could then have known that in less than a year's time three of the band would no longer be with us, and that 'Freebird' would be an elegy for singer Ronnie Van Zant, guitarist Steve Gaines and his backing-singer sister Cassie.

*Michael Heatley Record Buyer and Music Collector 1 April 02*

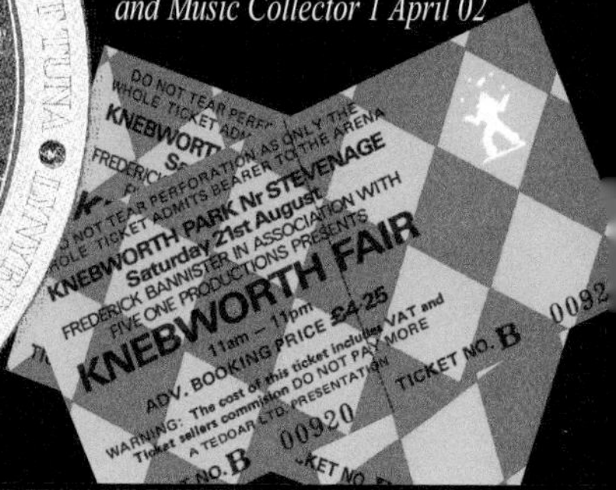

*Knebworth House Visitor's Book*

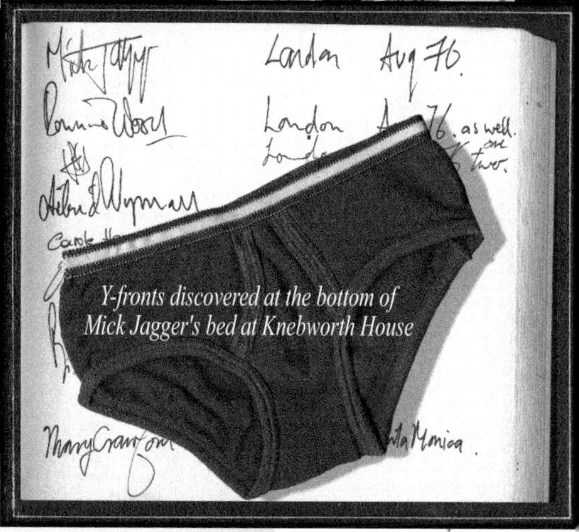


*Y-fronts discovered at the bottom of Mick Jagger's bed at Knebworth House*

JAGGER STILL PACKS THEM IN AT 33...

Asked if he was going to promote another event on this scale next year, Bannister, sweating, flustered but nevertheless apparently still in control, said: "How do you top the Stones?" *News of the World 22 August 76*

*Unofficial*

*Official*

# KNEBWORTH '78

## STAGE SET FOR WORLD RECORD

Everything in popular music always seems to be described in terms of the world's biggest, brightest or best. So now welcome what is claimed to be the world's largest stage. Over the last four weeks it has gradually taken shape in the grounds of Knebworth House, for this weekend's one-day rock concert featuring Genesis and Jefferson Starship. It is 75 yards wide, 25 yards deep and 60 feet high and concert organisers reckon the giant edifice deserves a place in the Guinness Book of Records. *James Johnson Evening Standard 23 June 78*

There was a shortlived nasty incident during the concert. A group called Demo (sic) appeared on the stage dressed in orange and white costumes. Their music obviously did not appeal and bottles and cans started to rain upon the stage. Privately, I was with the audience. They looked and sounded like demented parrots. *G. A. Pruette Licensing Officer*

"We are what a group is and must be at this point of time in order to follow the ritual of what a group represents and what it can do. " *Jerry Casale, Devo*

A fanfare introduced the Atlanta Rhythm Section. The fanfare was identified as the theme from Gone With The Wind, a most appropriate selection. A stiff breeze struck across the face of the stage, whipping the sound away from us towards Stevenage.

*Allan Jones Melody Maker 1 July 78*

During the interval a tatty looking character shambled on to the stage and unburdened himself of several deeply depressing dirges. One was called "I hate the white man". I never discovered why. To the crowd, cold, cocooned in polythene it was the last straw and they started throwing objects into the air. Everything went, clothes, cans, beach balls, balloons (where on earth did they come from?). Rolls and rolls of toilet paper shot up into the air. It was an astonishing sight.... I think the music was generally up to standard. Although I am not competent to judge, for I am tone deaf where pop music is concerned, the lyrics (if such they be) are, to me, incomprehensible. I paid particular attention to one number. It sounded like not so much a love song as detailed instructions in the art of Karate; in Japanese. *G. A. Pruette Licensing Officer*

# THE TIMES... THEY ARE A-CHANGING

The uniform of battered blue denim is still the same. But the people inside it are changed - not least around the middle. They have grown up, it seems, grown out and quietened down... The hair was shorter this time and the bra-less breasts were in the minority. Thousands of Saturday's paying customers (£5.50 and £6 a time) were definitely on the wrong side of 30. *Paul Donovan Daily Mirror 26 June 78*

I did discern a subtle change, fewer of the lunatic fringe, slightly older, some even had their hair cut short (both sexes) - the concert is obviously becoming an event, described by some as the Glyndebourne of the pop world. *G. A. Pruette Licensing Officer*

At last Genesis sallied onto "the world's largest ever stage" clad in glittering white suits. The intense blue glow of flash-lights erupted in erratic pin points of light all over the arena. The colossal battery of lamps burst into action. Brilliant lights shone from every corner, changing colour every few seconds. Vast revolving mirrors slowly moved over the stage intensifying the dazzling lights. Laser beams darted across the instruments and out into the sky in pencil streaks and scatter shots. Amplifiers stepped up the guitars and drums until the very towers of Knebworth House reverberated with the shock waves of sound and light. Eyes and ears were hypnotised. I know of nothing to equal it since the artillery barrage at the crossing of the Rhine. *G. A. Pruette Licensing Officer*

Equally impressive was the tolerance and good nature of the audience, and bearing in mind the bleak weather, their stoicism. They came, they heard, they saw, they went - quietly. *G. A. Pruette Licensing Officer*

# KNEBWORTH '78

## KNEBWORTH GOES DOWN THE TUBES

Yes, it's the excessive American TV quiz show, with a token rock legend and the best of British rock. *NME 16 September 78*

Re Styles... her snakey sinuous dancing was a turn on even at 300 yards.

*Phil Sutcliffe SOUNDS 16 September 78*

Yes, would you believe... when The Tubes sang the last choruses of "White Punks on Dope" there must have been 40 people on stage including a chorus line of dancing girls and a deputation of Salvation Army bandsmen (or close facsimiles). It was ridiculous and superb in its way, Billy Smart meets the Emperor Nero. The Christians and the lions both wore red noses and laughed at each other. *Phil Sutcliffe SOUNDS 16 September 78*

I called the festival 'Not Another Boring Old Knebworth'... in part to counter the criticism that the Knebworth Festivals and other large-scale events such as the recent appearance by Bob Dylan at Blackbush Airfield, had been receiving from some of the music journalists. They felt, it seemed, that these festivals featuring 'boring old dinosaurs' were rapidly becoming a musical irrelevance. *Freddy Bannister*

As before, the audience had the overall appearance of voluntary tramps of our affluent society. Jeans in every state of bleach and fade, many in terminal stages of wear, tattered in the leg, worn and patched everywhere. Studded, chain decked and beaten-up looking leather jackets. Sartorial elegance of the 70s? Or a means of asserting individuality?...

"D'ya know what this place reminds me of? A zoo - an expensive zoo. It's a rat-trap and you've all been conned!"

*Bob Geldof*

One young lady in clothing that was reckless and topless caught my eye - well - both eyes. I thought that she gave me such a look as I had not received for years until I realised that it was a musical facial twitch and that it was unlikely that she would find a bald ageing Local Government Officer an object of sensuous desire.

One group had the unappealing name of "The Boom Town Rats"... My only knowledge of the artist named "Zappa" was that during a London performance (for reasons unknown to me) he took off his trousers, apparently to the delight of the audience and consternation of the management... In the event it turned out to be the most placid concert of the series.

*G.A. Pruette, Licensing Officer*

# KNEBWORTH '79

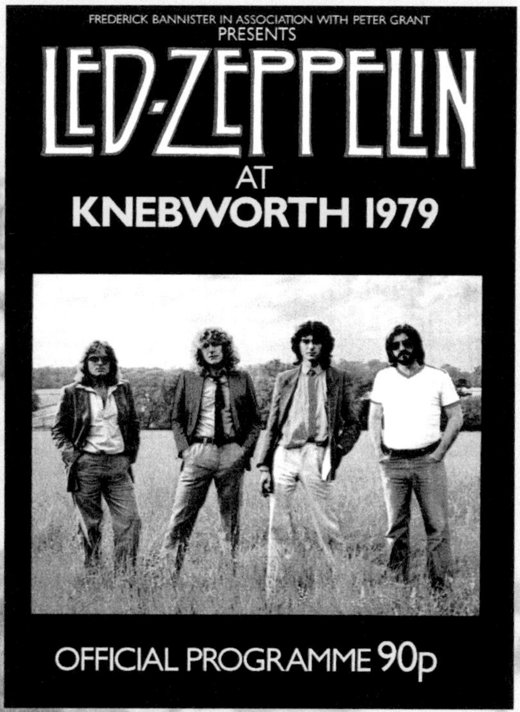


## THE KNEBWORTH FESTIVAL HAS BECOME THE ULTIMATE BRITISH ROCK AND ROLL EGO TRIP

I can think of very few bands who wouldn't give their eye teeth to stand where Led Zeppelin were standing last Saturday night... *Hugh Fielder Melody Maker 11 August 79*

"Well, I'm looking forward to... to Knebworth, actually. We've done a lot of rehearsing and checked things out. We've actually been down there and worked things out relative to the actual site. But then again it's like a natural amphitheatre so I imagine it's actually quite a good gig to be at..." *Jimmy Page, August 1979 (as quoted in "Follow the Legend")*

Just past the estate church... we were amused to see all four members of Zeppelin standing in line having their photograph taken by Storm Thorgerson, from Hipgnosis. Next to him, posturing for all she was worth, was a naked young woman obviously placed their by Storm to make the band less concious of the camera... After the session when the photographs were processed it was decided that the sky was not sufficiently blue and Storm...was sent out to Texas to take photos of proper blue skies that were later superimposed onto the Knebworth shots. *Freddy Bannister*

They played for more than three hours and finished with a fantastic version of Stairway to Heaven, during which the audience themselves became part of the show by holding aloft anything that would burn including cigarette lighters, matches, rolled up newspapers, even flags. An amazing sight. After this they played three well-deserved encores before calling it a day. By now it was 1.00am and we were once again in breach of licence. *Freddy Bannister*

Led Zeppelin at Knebworth were A Triumph... over 140,000 people can't be wrong. And neither can I. *Paul Morley New Musical Express 11 August 79*

...it took Led to lift the roof off... One to tell your grandchildren about." *Robin Smith Record Mirror 11 August 79*

Once the dust has died down nobody's going to remember how good or bad the band were; they will simply bounce young punks on their knees and recall the time they saw Led Zeppelin at Knebworth... *Hugh Fielder Melody Maker 11 August 79*

| | | | |
|---|---|---|---|
| Sandwiches | 30p | Doughnuts | 10p |
| Pasties | 20p | Pizzas | 65p |
| Sausage Rolls | 18p | Fish & Chips | 70p |
| Pork Pies | 30p | Chicken & Chips | 75p |
| Fruit Pies | 30p | Loose sweets | 20p quarter |
| Choc Rolls | 12p | Ice Creams Tonibell | |
| Drinks | 22p | Strawberry Treat | |
| Tea | 15p | Drink on a Stick | |
| Coffee | 18p | Vanilla Choc Ice | 15p |
| Soup | 15p | Frost Bar | 10p |
| Beef Burgers | 65p | Soft Ice Cream | 15p |
| Hot Dogs | 30p | Yoglace (Iced Yoghurt) | 15p |
| Hamburgers | 35p | Yoghurt | 15p |

Afterwards the band went up to Knebworth House for a drink. Peter (Grant, Zeppelin's manager) was at his arrogant best... (telling David Lytton Cobbold) that his own house Horselunges Manor was grade one listed and that Knebworth House as far as he knew was only grade two. *Freddy Bannister*

*Freddy Bannister*

## DEBTS £250,000: ASSETS £7,000 BANNISTER'S KNEBWORTH DISASTER

The massive debts of rock concert promoter Fred Bannister were revealed at a creditor's meeting this week... *Welwyn Times 21 September 79*

## KNEBWORTH: IS THIS THE END?

Promoter Fred Bannister has put his company Teodoar Ltd. into liquidation following the two festivals with Led Zeppelin in August. *Sounds 22 September 79*

## STATELY HOME OWNER FACES THE MUSIC

The owner of stately Knebworth House has paid the penalty for allowing an open-air concert to rock-on beyond its midnight deadline. David Lytton Cobbold admitted breaking a condition of a music and dance licence when he appeared in court at Stevenage in Hertfordshire, yesterday. He was fined £125 and £25 costs... *Express and Star 11th December 79*

Do I miss the music business? Of course; I miss the people, the humour, the camaraderie. Above all I miss the great music, but come to think of it doesn't everyone?

*Freddy Bannister There Must Be A Better Way 2001*

# KNEBWORTH '80

## GOOD VIBRATIONS FOR THE AGEING TRENDIES *Welwyn Times 2 May 80*

We thought our chances of getting another licence were fairly slim, but when Capital Radio and J. Lyons, a subsidiary of Allied Breweries, approached us with an offer we thought it worth a try. We obtained a licence for 100,000 but only after assurances to the Council that the consortium running the event, Capital Radio, Allied Breweries and Andy Hudson Promotions, would pay all the bills and stop the music on time. A bond of £25,000 was held by the Council which would go to a charity if the concert ran over. *Chryssie Lytton Cobbo*

In case you're wondering why we aren't covering Knebworth, well we didn't think you'd be interested in the antics of a lot of boring old has-beens. *NME 28 June 80*

Crowds at Saturday's rock festival in Knebworth, Herts, may be "bombed"... with 5,000 ping-pong balls. London's Capital Radio has applied to the Civil Aviation Authority for permission to stage the stunt from a B17 bomber to "keep the crowds happy". *Oldham Evening Chronicle 18 June 1980*

*Beach Boy Al Jardine on the roof of Knebworth House*

# ROCKIN' IN THE TREETOPS

Battier doings than usual will be evident at this year's Knebworth pop festival, where an American professor plans to test the effect of the music on local trees. Professor Jackson is hoping to clamber up two similar trees, one close to the festival's loudspeakers and the other a mile or two away... to monitor the progess of the leaves. *The Guardian 12 June 80*

Looking out over the thousands of blissfully happy fans at Knebworth streaming back to their tents as the last echoes of the Beach Boy's "Fun Fun Fun" died away, it occured to me that all of us, whether old-style ageing hippies like myself or the younger puritans of the new wave, ought to stop bad-mouthing mega-festivals like this for not being what they were never intended to be: the adolescent quasi-political fantasies of Abbie Hoffman and his "Woodstock Nation"... Knebworth Nation does not exist. What does exist, although we try to deny it, is an audience that actually likes what used to be called a tribal gathering: a place to picnic, listen to famous names re-living their vinyl triumphs, have a bit of a cuddle, smoke a bit of grass, drink a lot of beer, put up an umbrella if it rains, and take off your jacket if the sun comes out.

*Karl Dallas Melody Maker 28 June 80*

*Carlos Santana*

*The Blues Band*

By eleven o'clock I was drenched in sweat and ready to drop, but the encore of "Good Vibrations" and "Fun Fun Fun" dragged the last drop of energy forth. I've never seen so many people dancing at one time and I've certainly never enjoyed a concert the way I enjoyed the final two hours of the 1980 Knebworth Festival. *Nick Kemp New Music News 28 June 80*

Economists will probably hail the 1980 Knebworth Pop Festival as something of a flop. The 50,000 crowd that turned up was just half the number promoters had hoped for and at best they will only break even. But the compensations may be greater. Not only did the fans enjoy a really tremendous day's music; but the promoter won praise and goodwill all round for successfully organising an event which has drawn so much criticism in past years. *Hitchin Gazette 26 June 80*

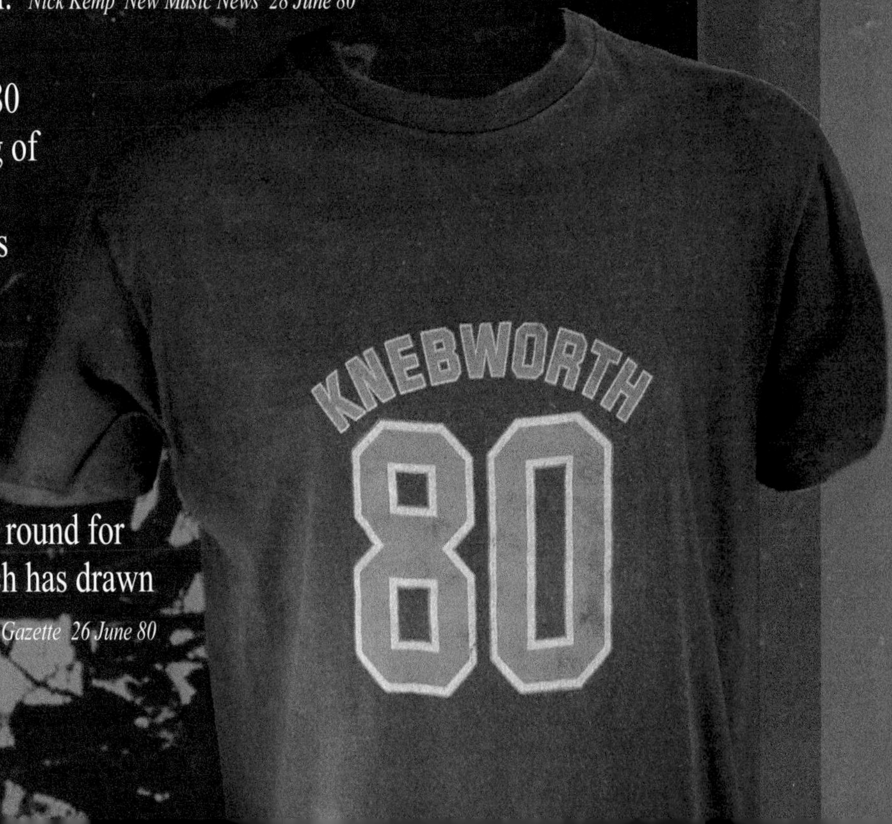

# KNEBWORTH '80 - '82

## WORLD'S LARGEST DISCO PLAN FOR KNEBWORTH PARK

A new idea to bring music loving youngsters to Knebworth has been born. London promoters have drawn up plans for the world's largest disco in a circus tent at the stately home. And they say 15,000 people could pack in to dance to top performers there in the spring. *Watford Evening Echo 4 October 7*

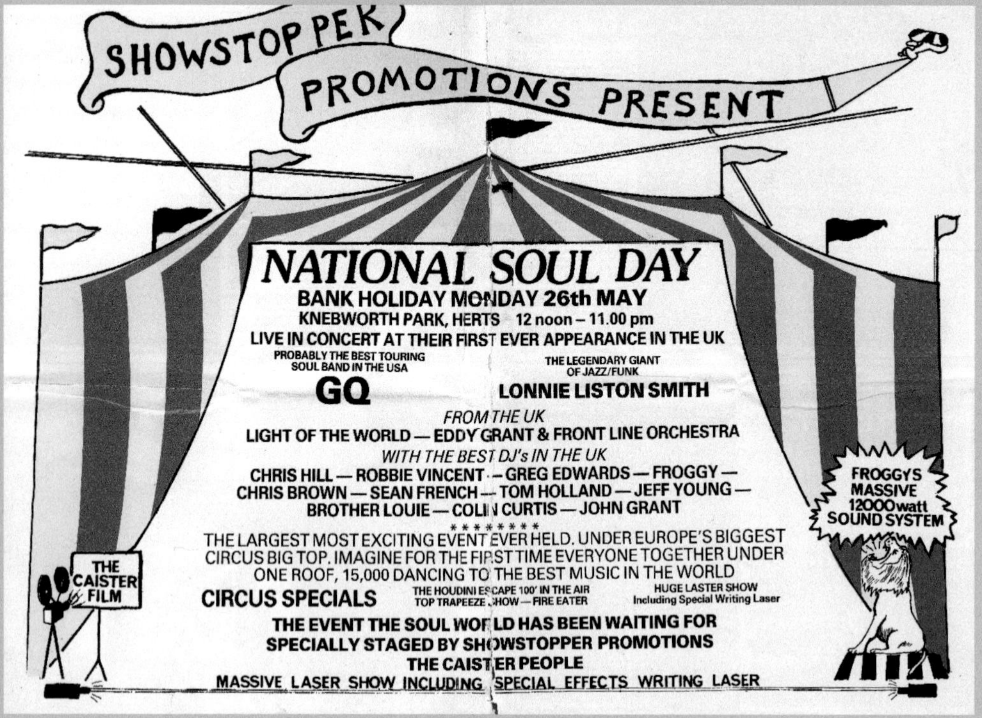


Europe's largest soul festival held at Knebworth Park was marred on Monday when violence erupted near the end. The worst trouble came just after 9pm when people queuing for over half an hour at catering stands pushed forward and hot dogs, drinks and ice cream were upset and stolen... Everyone will talk about the violence and vandalism that tainted the festival but it should be remembered that nearly all those who went had the time of their lives...

*Nick Rines Hitchin Gazette 29 May 80*

## SUCCESS FOR 1ST ALTERNATIVE FESTIVAL

Knebworth Park is more used to visiting megastars like the Beach Boys and the Rolling Stones, but last week it was unknowns who got their chance to shine.

*Welwyn and Hatfield Times June 11 81*

*local fan, Kim Wilde*

## ALTERNATIVE KNEBFEST RIDES AGAIN

*Welwyn Times 27 August 82*

Punk chartbusters 23 Skidoo have been signed to headline the 2nd Alternative Music Festival at stately Knebworth Park

## PIKESTAFFS AND PUNK STUFF

Punks and pikemen were tying themselves in knots on Sunday as the safety pin brigade and a civil war society headed for Knebworth to enjoy the sun... The punks were outnumbered, and often outdressed, by the Royalists and the Roundhea who were staging a moc battle to entertain the holiday crow

*Hitchin Gazette 3 June*

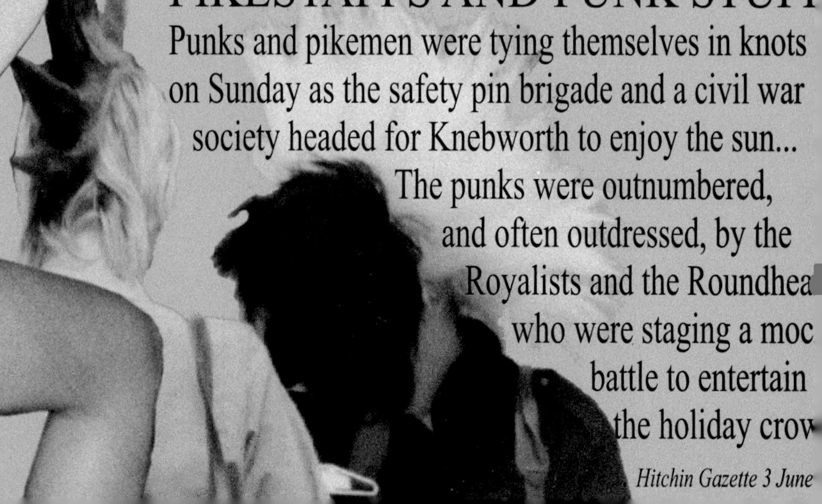

he punks were here to hear 11 ew wave ands and enjoy he Alternative nebworth estival...

# JAZZ STARS MOVE TO KNEBWORTH AFTER RIOT FEARS

Knebworth Park has come to the rescue of a major jazz festival. Knebworth was picked out by the festival's promoter's, Capital Radio, after they quit original venue, Clapham Common, on police advice... *David Faers Welwyn Times 24 July 81*

*Ella Fitzgerald signs David Lytton Cobbold's favourite album (after "Dark Side of the Moon"!)*

## ELLA'S MAGIC WOOS THE JAZZ FANS

Picnic tables creaked laden with wine bottles and quiches. Families with deck chairs and prams rubbed shoulders with middle-aged couples with shooting sticks and hampers. Everyone had come well prepared for what turned out to be the most up-market festival yet. The traditional invasion of denim-clad rock fans was replaced by a quiet influx of mature, even elderly connoisseurs of jazz. Sports jackets, comfy cords and smart wellies were the order of the day, blending perfectly with the stately surroundings.

*Judy Jones North Herts Gazette Series (no date)*

**PROGRAMME 18TH JULY**
THE BASIE ALUMNI
CHUCK BERRY
MORRISSEY/MULLEN BAND
LARRY CORYELL
BOB CROSBY & THE ORIGINAL BOBCATS
MEL TORME TRIO
RONNIE SCOTT
CHICK COREA
DOROTHY DONEGAN
GEORGIE FAME
**PROGRAMME 19TH JULY**
CONCORD ALL STARS
SHELLY MANNE
LEE KONITZ
BOBBY LAMB/RAY PREMRU BIG BAND
STAN TRACEY
MILT HINTON
DIZZY GILLESPIE ALL STARS
TEDDY WILSON
ROSS TOMPKINS
HERBIE HANCOCK QUARTET
SHAKATAK
THE INVERSIONS
**SITE PLAN**
**PROGRAMME 25TH JULY**
ELLA FITZGERALD/JIMMY ROW
BUDDY DE FRANCO/TERRY GIBB
McCOY TYNER AND FRIENDS
DEXTER GORDON
ART PEPPER
TRUMMY YOUNG
PIZZA EXPRESS ALL STARS
PETE ALLEN JAZZ BAND
NYJO
BARBARA THOMPSON'S PARAPH
**PROGRAMME 26TH JULY**
MAJOR HOLLEY'S
TRIBUTE TO LOUIS JORDAN
SARAH VAUGHAN
RICHIE COLE
MUDDY WATERS
GEORGE MELLY
JOHN CHILTON
HUMPHREY LYTTELTON
ZOOT MONEY
RED RODNEY/IRA SULLIVAN
JAZZ ON CAPITAL

ARTIST. LIONEL HA
PERFORMANCE TIME 8.30

ARTIST. SARAH VAUG
PERFORMANCE TIME 7.30

ARTIST. HERBIE HANCOCK
PERFORMANCE TIME

*Muddy Waters*

ARTIST. ELLA FITZGERALD
PERFORMANCE TIME 6.45

ARTIST. DEXTER GORDON
PERFORMANCE TIME 9.00

*Required 1980s Stage Manager attire...*

# KNEBWORTH '82

## JAZZ FESTIVAL SELL-OUT... AT LAST

Organisers of the Capital Radio Jazz Festival at Knebworth, had to close the gates six hours before music stopped last Saturday. The reason? For the first time in its four-year history, the festival was a sell-out, with 15,000 making their way to Knebworth - despite the train strike... *Letchworth and Baldock Citizen 22 July 82*

# HOURS OF BLAZING SUNSHINE AND ALL THAT JAZZ

Day One of the Capital Jazz Festival - a day when musical barriers meant nothing and thousands of people enjoyed a heady mixture of jazz, Jamaican reggae, American blues and British soul. The musical pot-pourri was a surefire recipe for success, attracting fans from every age group and income bracket. They danced, drank, sang and made merry as blazing sunshine turned the Knebworth Park arena into a giant frying pan full of sizzling, sun burned bodies. The gently rolling hill-sides - just in sight of the stately home - made a perfect natural amphitheatre and Capital surrounded it with an impressive aray of PA hardware. *David Faers Welwyn and Hatfield Times*

In this space, it is impossible to descibed adequately the joy, the artistry and, most important of all, the sheer catholic taste and good-natured vibes of the first weekend of the Capital Radio Jazz Festival at Knebworth Park. Buckton's sad army had done their best to keep the crowds away, but 18,000 turned up on Sunday for a feast of music in the balmy Hertfordshire air, with that dreamlike Gothic fantasy of Knebworth House within view to persuade them it wasn't happening. Happening it was, though, and how Capital deserved their luck after the dreadful years of fire and race riots they've endured. *Derek Jewel The Sunday Times 25 July 82*

CAPITAL RADIO
JAZZ
FESTIVAL '82

PRESENTED BY CAPITAL RADIO
IN ASSOCIATION WITH CHILTERN RADIO

# KNEBWORTH '82 - '83

## ROCKING IN THE NAME OF THE LORD

The Guardian 29 Aug 83

Around 20,000 fans from all over the world came and went over the four days. A creche was provided for younger listeners. Unemployed people were entitled to 50% off the ticket price. It was so peaceful that four policemen turned up and two went home. *Chryssie Lytton Cobbold*

The organisers were keen to come again the following year. 1983 was the Christian Green Belt Festival's tenth anniversary and Cliff Richard would head the music bill. They expected about 45,000 people over the whole weekend.

The weekend was hot and sunny and the next crisis was over the water supply. Pop fans come and go without much need of water, but Christians need flush loos, water for washing themselves and their dishes and even nappies which hung on lines strung between tent poles to dry. Our own water tank, supplied by the mains, dried up.

Strict music and dancing laws apply on Sundays in Hertfordshire, and all noise must stop by 10.30 p.m. Fairly certain that in spite of this being a Christian Festival, they would not stop at 10.30, David and I went down to the main stage at about 10.25 p.m. Sure enough a religious musical was in full progress with no sign of finishing in five minutes. We searched everywhere for the Stage Manager and eventually found him cuddling his girlfriend under the stage. The play started late due to an electrical fault and was only half way through; no way could he stop it and in spite of our protests he didn't. Luckily none of the licensing officers were around.

ou won't forget our 10 year special...

KNEBWORTH PARK, HERTS
26TH ~ 29TH AUGUST 1983

"Greenbelt has proved immensely valuable time and again as a spring-board for ideas, a pool for opinions, a channel of truth"
SUE GERRARD

"I always really enjoy Greenbelt and always return home marvellously refreshed, even if a little sleepy!"
NICK LEWIS

"Over the past couple of years I've been taking small groups of lads to the Greenbelt Festival from Portland Borstal, with some truly amazing and long lasting results – Praise the Lord!"
ANDREW MARSDEN
Chaplain Portland Borstal

"We have been coming as a family with our 3 young children for the last 5 years. Our youngest came as a baby of only 3 months."
BERYL & REX from Derby

"I thought it was going to be like any other Outside Broadcast. When I got there I thought this is the most enormous sort of Holiday Park. I mean there were tents and thousands and thousands of people. I was absolutely astounded by the reaction that people gave to me and the warmth and generous hospitality. I thought it was going to be very docile, very homely affair – little did I know that it was going to be the most amazing reaction I've ever faced."
PETER POWELL Radio 1 DJ

GREENBELT '83

BOOKED SO FAR:

om the UK- CLIFF RICHARD & BAND • MARK WILLIAMSON
GARTH HEWITT • 100% PROOF • SHEILA WALSH
ARITY • GEOFFREY STEVENSON & GRAHAM KENDRICK
EANNE HINTON • DR JOHN STOTT • JUNE OSBORNE
AT BAND • ECHOES OF JOY • FOOTPRINTS • SPRINGS
CORNERSTONE • EARLY WARNING (featuring Alexander John)
from America- MARIA MULDAUR • MIGHTY CLOUDS OF JOY
LLOYD BLUE • ANDY PRATT • ROBIN LANE
ANDY STONEHILL • KENNY MARKS • JERRY ARHELGER
AC FRAMPTON • MAC & THE BEES • RICHARD FOSTER
from Sweden- JERUSALEM • DYNAMIS from Holland- THEO LENS
from Ireland- RODNEY CORDNER from Germany- SEMAJA
om Africa - CEASAR MOLEBATSI PLUS OUR REGULARS- JOHN ALLEN, PIP WILSON, GRAHAM CRAY, JOHN PECK, ANDREW KIRK & ALLEN and ELEANOR KREIDER
PLUS- MANY OTHER MAJOR ATTRACTIONS STILL TO BE ANNOUNCED...

printed 5 months before the event. For all the 'latest' - phone the GB 'Hotline' 01-740-0433 for our 24hr news message.

MEMORANDUM

| From | To |
|---|---|
| Dawn | David Cobbold |

REF. SUBJECT Greenbelt DATE 28th August

I thought you might be interested to know that there have been several complaints about the noise from the Greenbelt Festival at unreasonable hours. Not least of which was the message left on the office ansafone this morning:-

"When is that ****** racket going to stop? I need to get some sleep. It's a ****** disgrace. Don't you dare let it happen again next year."

Unfortunately this call was anonymous so we will be unable to contact the gentleman concerned to apologise.

Dawn

By Monday night, four continuous days of incredibly loud, and often bad, music had exhausted our patience and all our neighbours' too. At 3 a.m. on Tuesday morning David, in his nightshirt, pulled the plug . Our popularity rating locally was nil. It was going to be difficult building our reputation again.

*Chryssie Lytton Cobbold*

# KNEBWORTH '85

## IT'S PURPLE RAIN!

It's going to take more than a little drop of rain to dampen the enthusiasm of the 80,000 rock fans who slipped and slithered their way into Knebworth Park last Saturday. For those who remember the Knebworth Festival as one of the most fantastic occasions on the music calendar, it was marvellous to see it bounce back to its best ever. *Mark Norman North Herts Gazette Series 28 June 85*

Known as "The Knebworth Fayre" and with Deep Purple heading the bill, the line-up also included Scorpions, Meat Loaf, UFO, Blackfoot, Mountain, Mama's Boys and Alaska. The date was June 22 and tickets were £14.00. It was to be Deep Purple's only 1985 appearance in Britain since re-forming the previous year. The biggest obstacle was a police bill estimated at £60,000... in desperation we took the police to Court, nine days before the Festival was due to open. The Judge decided that on points of law the police won. So there we were, eight days before the concert, with no licence... *Chryssie Lytton Cobbold*

But by this time the attendance looked to be under 75,000, so the police dropped their charges to £30,000.

Advertisements and posters read "No camping, no bottles, no cameras, no tapes etc". I felt like adding "no fun". *Chryssie Lytton Cobbold*

urtesy of The Connoisseur Collection and Simon Robinson*

# MUD-WORTH...

The weather went from bad to worse, and the mud was a nightmare... There followed an exhausting night, trying to get everyone out of the mud. Farmers came with their tractors and worked until morning, pulling cars and coaches out of the quagmire. *Chryssie Lytton Cobbold*

But on the whole it was a great day, hopefully heralding the start of a new era of Knebworth Festivals. *Peterborough Evening Telegraph 28 June 85*

*Meatloaf*

# RACKET COSTS A PACKET

Lord Cobbold's heir, David Lytton Cobbold, has paid the price for the ear-shattering din at his Gothic monstrosity Knebworth House, Herts, during a pop festival last summer. The heavy metal groups Deep Purple and Meatloaf well exceeded sound limits set by North Herts District council. Now local magisatrates have fined him £500. *Daily Express 24 January 86*

# KNEBWORTH '86

*ourtesy of Queen Productions Ltd*

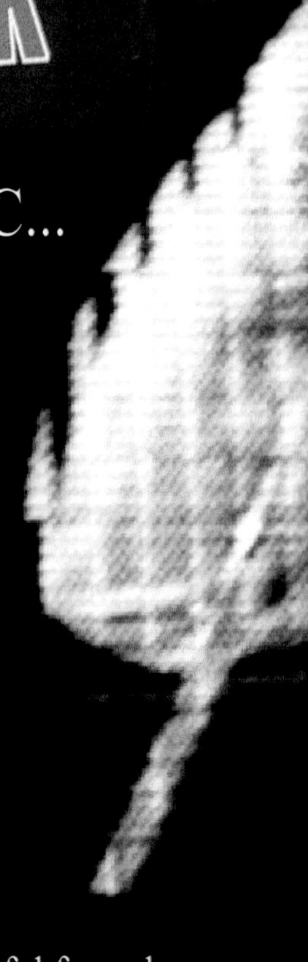

A KIND OF MAGIC...

Their rock and roll highnesses reigned supreme over 120,000 subjects at Knebworth Park on Saturday...

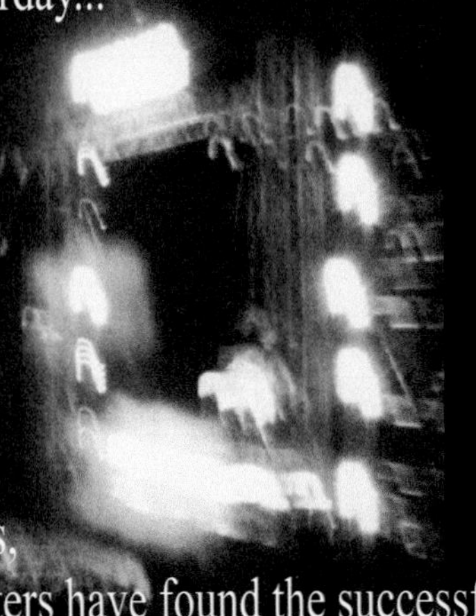

Happily and gloriously they churned out hit after hit and the crowds, stretching as far as the eye can see, joined in. It was the best run concert ever held at Knebworth and for that the organisers, the performers and the crowd, must take credit. At last the promoters have found the successful formula.

*Rick Cowdery North Herts Gazette Series 15 August 86*

## VENUE FIT FOR QUEEN *Newcastle Journal 9 July 86*

Knebworth House, the Glyndebourne of rock, plays host to the biggest rock concert in Britain tomorrow (Saturday) since Bob Dylan topped the bill on the Isle of Wight. Queen, rated the best rock band in the world today, round off a European tour which has seen them play to more than one million people in eight different countries.

*North Herts Gazette Series 8 August 86*

## QUEEN CONCERT ENDS IN DEATH...

A 21-year-old man was killed early yesterday during a huge open air concert by top rock band Queen. He was stabbed repeatedly as he listened to the group. Four men have been detained.

*Northern Echo 11 August 86*

# KNEBWORTH '90

## DINOSAURS ROAM THE PARK

*James Rampton The Independant on Sunday 24 June 90*

Isn't that Eric on guitar? And Knopfler? And Elton on piano... indeed it was - and this was just one item on the most stella musical bill since Live Aid. *Mat Snow Q Aug 90* The "rock wrinklies" turned out in their tens of thousands yesterday to bring back the memories listening to a galaxy of stars... The throng of 125,000 had helped raise £6 million for charity... The stars were ferried in and out of the arena by a fleet of 20 helicopters. Each performer had his own dressing room in a mock-up of London's Hard Rock Cafe... The money raised will pay for a new £3 million home for the Nordoff-Robbins Music Therapy Centre for handicapped children. Another £3 million will go to a new London School for Performing Arts and Technology.

*Henry Macrory and Ian Henry London Evening Standard 25 June 90*

*"We had a brilliant day. By the time we took the stage it was nice and dark - and when the rain came back it made things very atmospheric for our lights and lasers"*
*Dave Gilmore*

## ROCK OF ALL AGES

Middle-aged couples in Barbour sweaters rubbed shoulders with teenagers in torn jeans and leather jackets as one-by-one the pop world's living legends climbed the massive high-tech Knebworth stage in a spectacular beamed to 65 countries around the world.

*Hugh Muir Mail on Sunday 1 July 90*

Nostalgists for the Floyd at Knebworth '75 might regret the curious lack of Spitfire flypast, but as the helicopters thump and chatter overhead in the eerily illuminated monsoon, few can doubt that here and now is the place to be. *Mat Snow Q Aug 90*

THE GREATEST SHOW ON EARTH *Billy Sloan Glasgow Daily Record 24 Oct 89*

# KNEBWORTH '92

"THIS IS A TRUE GENESIS AUDIENCE -
NO COOL PEOPLE WHATSOEVER" *Phil Collins*

New Age travellers in converted ice cream vans were distinctly lacking. There were however plenty of gleaming Peugeot 205s and crisply ironed t-shirts, many bearing the dates of past Genesis tours...

At 8.30pm, an age old rock concert tradition was shattered when the main act took the stage precisely on time. (Blame live coverage on radio and TV). *Steve Punt Sunday Times 9 August 92*

In May this year, I was flicking through Radio Times when I came across a full-colour advert for Genesis at Knebworth, "sponsored by Volkswagen". Suddenly the full horror of being almost 30 hit me... The last time Genesis played Knebworth I was 15, and the full-page ads were in smudgy black-and-white in Melody Maker... In 1978, to get to Knebworth from the Home Counties meant a stop-start crawl through London. In 1992, it means a stop-start crawl around the M25. The Department of Transport, obviously forewarned that 70,000 people were converging on Stevenage, had thoughtfully arranged some faulty traffic lights at South Mimms, and the A1 was reduced by mass columns of cones to roughly the width of a cart-track. *Steve Punt Sunday Times 9 August 92*

# '95

## THE BANK THAT LIKES TO SAY 'YO' *The Times 17 March 95*

It had to happen: rock music has joined the grown-up art forms such as opera, symphony music, blockbuster art exhibitions and the rest. Lloyds Bank is to sponsor the Glyndebourne of rock, Knebworth, to the tune of £1m...

## ROCK SHOW SHOCKER

The biggest event of the year the Knebworth Festival has been scrapped. The open-air show, scheduled for July 1st, was to feature the cream of British rock playing to an audience of 120,000. It was expected to raise about £5m for charity. *Daily Mirror 24 March 95*

Promoter and chairman of the Nordoff Robbins music charity, Andrew Miller, says, "We have taken a responsible decision to reschedule the concert to next year when we can announce a bill worthy of the Knebworth tradition." *Music Week 1 April 95*

# KNEBWORTH '96

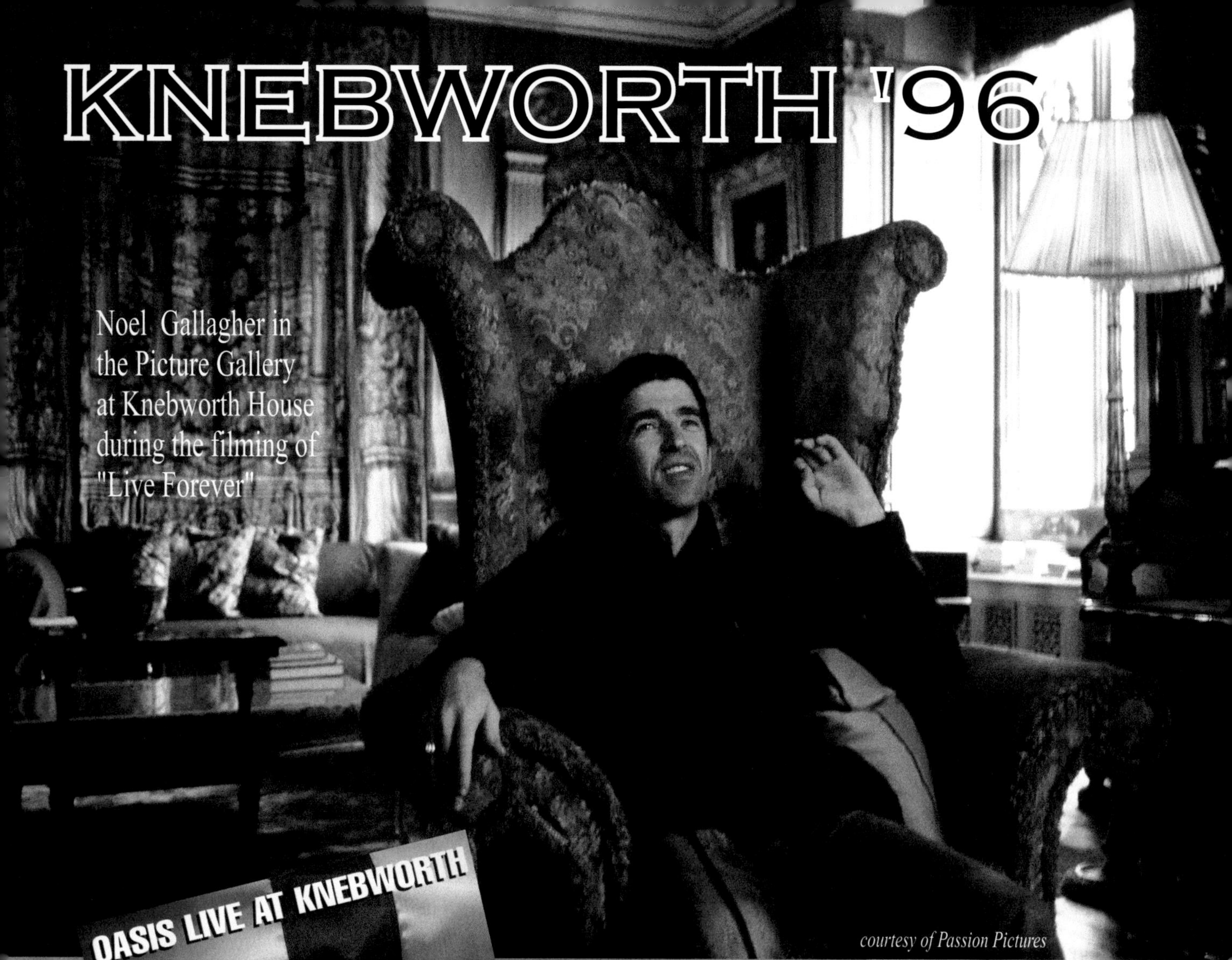

Noel Gallagher in the Picture Gallery at Knebworth House during the filming of "Live Forever"

*courtesy of Passion Pictures*

Noel remembers being served champagne by a liveried servant while lounging in the bath of Knebworth House the next day. *Sunday Times Magazine 18 June 00*

*The "liveried servant" was actually Lord Cobbold. Noel signs the Knebworth House guest book "Clean". His minder signs "Dirty".*

10/11 August - Oasis Concert
Sally Christensen Dittisham, Devon Memorable!
11. AUGUST. NOEL GALLAGHER (OASIS) clean!!
Sean Rufus Rogg dirty!!!

# OASIS IN CONCERT SELL-OUT SCORCHER IT'S GIG-ANTIC! *News of the World 11 Aug 96*

Oasis sold all 330,000 tickets for its summer shows in just nine hours, it was disclosed yesterday – a rate of more than twenty ticket sales a second. *Glasgow Herald 14 May 96*

"There's big, then there's bigger than big, and then there's last night. Now that is big." Noel on the first night of Knebworth. *Select Oct 96*

"Has God played Knebworth recently?" Noel, later.

"All the people... so many people..." Liam Gallagher, first night.

"(Best moment of the 90s?) Getting married was great. And then Knebworth, all them people there and up for it, that's what I'd always wanted to do, a big gathering like that in a nice place." Liam Gallagher, later.

"This is going out live.. so shit, fuck and bum." Noel, live.

"I queued all night for my ticket to Knebworth", said Pete Irving, 28, still clutching the priceless scrap of paper as if it might be snatched away. "I knew this would be something I could tell my kids about in years to come. Of course I can't even see the band it's so crowded, I'm just watching the screens. But the point is, I was here."
Victoria Coren Daily Mail 12 August 96

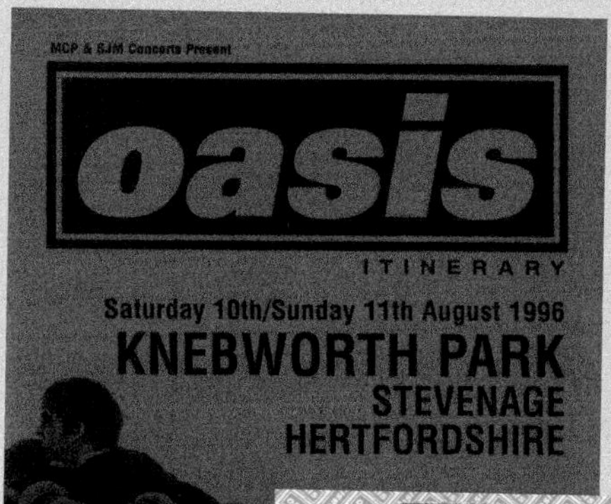

oasis
KNEBWORTH PARK
SATURDAY 10TH AUGUST 1996
SHOWTIMES

DOORS:

| | |
|---|---|
| THE BOOTLEG BEATLES | 1400 - 1430 |
| CHEMICAL BROTHERS | 1500 - 1545 |
| Ocean Colour Scene | 1615 - 1700 |
| MANIC STREET PREACHERS | 1730 - 1830 |
| prodigy | 1900 - 2000 |
| oasis | 2045 - 2245 |
| CURFEW: | 2300 |

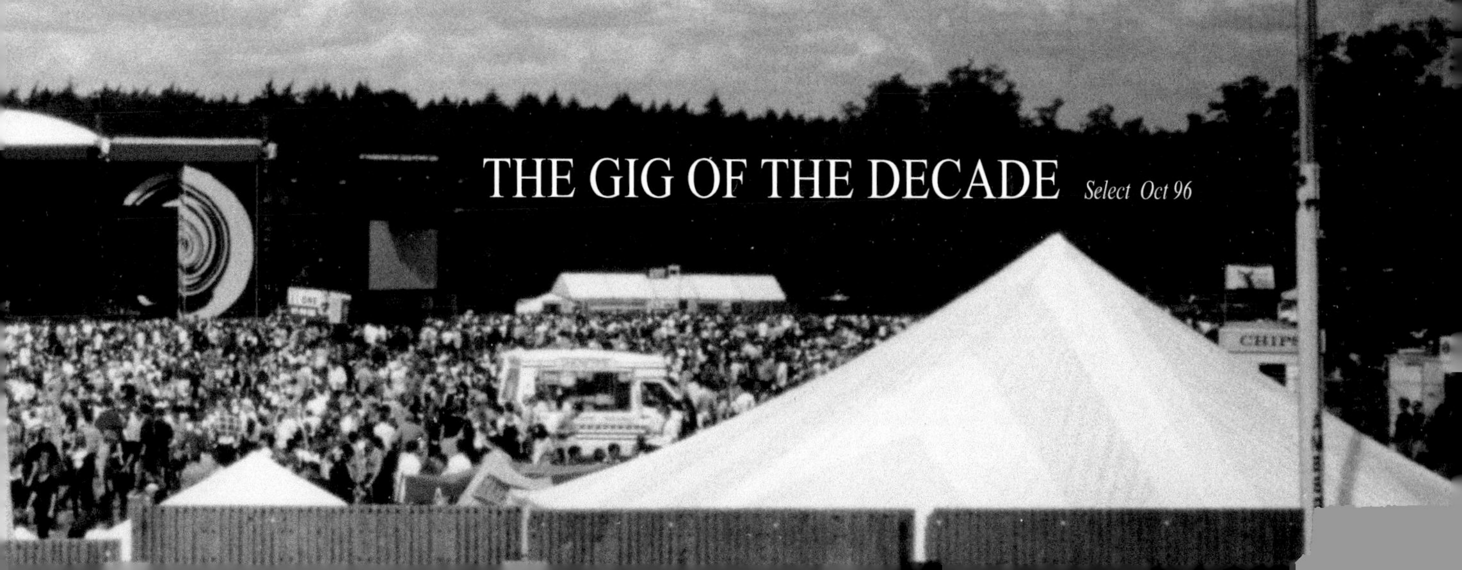

THE GIG OF THE DECADE *Select Oct 96*

# KNEBWORTH '01

## CLUBBERS STORM ROCK STRONGHOLD

For people who need proof that dance music is the stongest force on the British music scene, here it is... *Richard Simpson Evening Standard 31 May 01*

Following the sell-out takeover of the Millennium Dome on New Year's Eve, Ministry of Sound is to stage a massive 50,000 capacity summer event featuring the world's biggest DJs and clubs. Taking place at Hertfordshire's Knebworth House - once host to some of the biggest rock spectaculars - the all night festival is expected to be one of Europe's biggest summer dance music events. Creative Director Mark Rodol says: "It'll unite all forms of dance music smack bang in the middle of summer - it's gonna be huge." *Ministry March 01*

*There had been previous attempts in the late 90s to bring dance festivals to Knebworth - they, like Ministry, all met with strong opposition from the neighbours...*

Dear Neighbour,

**I am writing to urge you to write to Lord & Lady Cobbold and the council to oppose this terrible festival they are trying to hold, Tribal Gathering.**

This is not a concert where people come for the day and then go home. This is for three days and goes on all night. It will be devastating on our village and our lives and our sleep.

**The traffic will be appalling.** This is a bank holiday weekend. The A1M is at full capacity at Bank Holidays on both the Friday and Saturday and cannot take extra traffic from such an event. Then the people are here for three days. What will happen? Will they be locked in? No of course not. You cannot keep them imprisoned and they will be in and out of the estate onto the A1M all night and day causing accidents or they will have to come out of the estate into our village. Neither option is acceptable and there is no way that they can keep them on the estate for such a long time without them leaving. The police could not keep them in for Oasis when they just forced their way out and they will not be able to keep them in on this one. The Chief Constable should resist this on our behalf and oppose this because of the dangers on the A1M. and in our village. It will be our worst nightmare.

**Noise,** the organisers have promised to be going all through the night. David Phillips from the promoters has been on Radio 1 telling everyone that it is going to be the biggest, loudest & wildest festival ever. We do not want that on our doorstep and disturbing our lives and our sleep. We have suffered during the daytime with concert noise from Knebworth and getting them to turn it down is almost impossible. This will be impossible and it will go through the night. It will be impossible to sleep. The council must protect us and stop this.

**Drugs,** the place will be awash with drugs. This is a Rave. Raves exist on drugs, The whole area will be awash with drugs and drug dealers. The Cobbold family should not allow this to happen to our village. At Glastonbury they fornicate & defecate in the gardens in the area and set up camp sites in peoples gardens. The organisers want to bring this sort of thing to our village with the Cobbolds consent. Why should we suffer this? Thousands turn up and walk around trying to get in. This is going to happen here. the police are powerless to stop it. When people turn up without tickets they will end up in our village.

**We must stop this awful rave now. The Cobbolds will not keep our support by bringing raves to the estate. Normal pop concerts are one thing but this is not acceptable.**

**Please write to the council to object. Address letters to Mr. Peters. Licensing, Town Hall, Broadway, Letchworth. These letters need to be in by this Monday 14th Dec.**

## Ministry end long wait

It's been a long wait but five years after Oasis rocked 250,000 at Knebworth Park, festival fever returns once again. With 150 DJs and dance acts it certainly represents a departure from Knebworth Festivals of old...

*Stevenage Comet 9 Aug 01*

Eleven huge arenas are being erected in the beautiful grounds of Knebworth Park for a whole spectrum of house, garage, trance, drum&bass and Balearic beats tomorrow. Jay Kay, lead singer of Jamiroquai, says: "We're really looking forward to playing outdoors at Knebworth, our first gig for over a year."

*Birmingham Evening Mail 10 Aug 01*

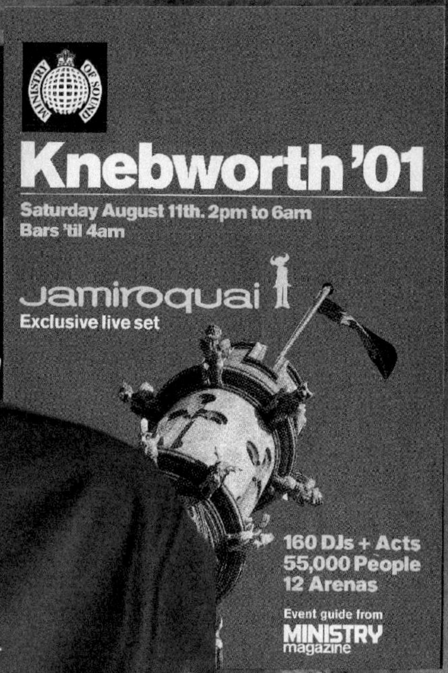


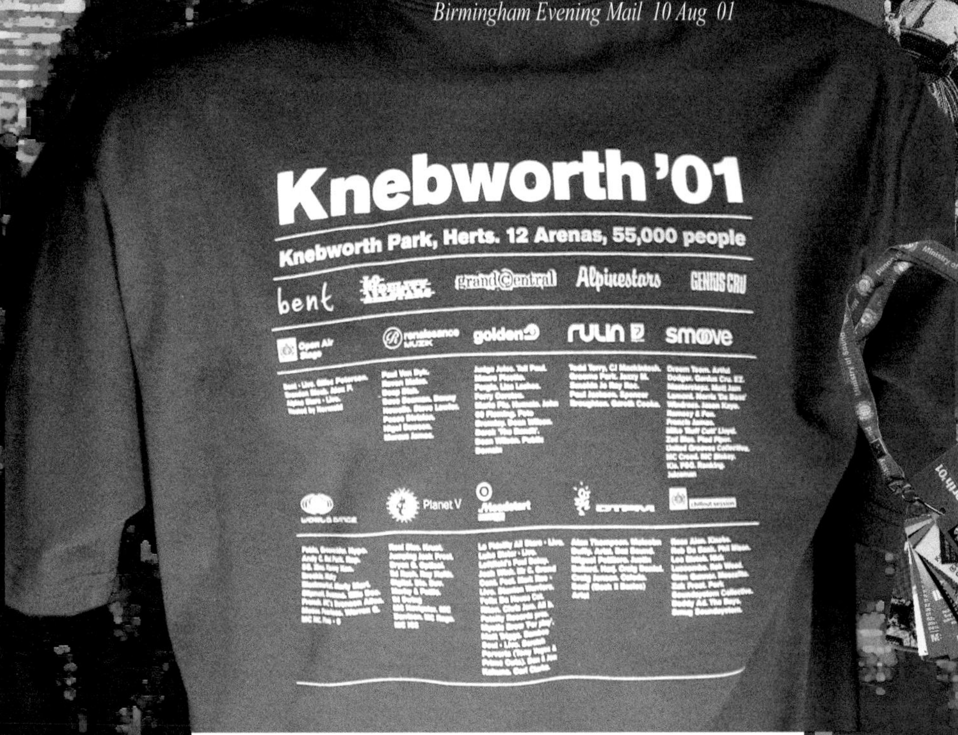


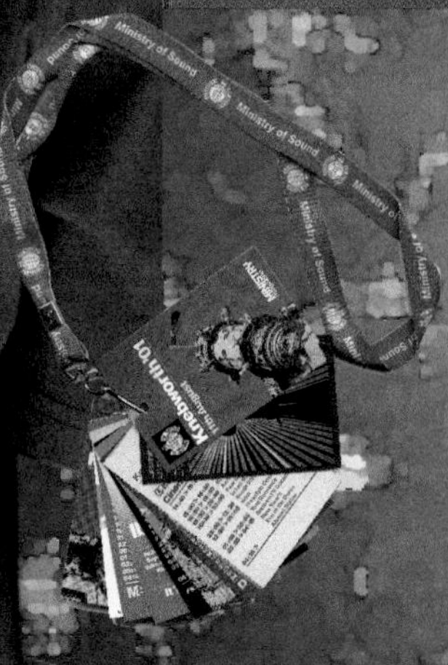

*"I'd like to thank the Earl of Knobworth for having such a big knob!" Jay Kay during the sound check... He was later introduced to David - now Lord Cobbold - "the one with the big knob". Jay blushed.*

*photo, interestingly, by Patti Clapton*

Mercifully the rain held off, except for a few drops in the early hours. But by then no-one cared. Those who saw it through until 6am trudged off with weary feet, but having witnessed what was surely one of the year's best parties.

*Paul Brackle Stevenage Mercury 17 Aug 01*

# KNEBWORTH '03

## *TAKE THIS...* *Shropshire Star 7 Dec 02*

*Robbie Williams is planning his biggest ever gig - at the scene of arch rivals Oasis' crowning glory. He will headline a four-day festival at Knebworth Park, Herts, next July... Knebworth became synonymous with Oasi when 250,000 fans piled into the park to pay homage to the group, who at the time were the biggest rock and roll band in the world. But the Gallagher brothers' popularity is waning and Robbie sees Knebworth as an opportunity to get one over on the Manchester lads who once branded him "a fat dancer from Take That".*

*The Sun 7 Nov 02*

*READY FOR ROBBIE TO ENTERTAIN YOU...*

*FULL HOUSES ALL AROUND AS COUNTDOWN BEGINS TO WILLIAMS INVASION... Hotels and supermarkets are bracing themselves for the Robbie Williams invasion - which is still EIGHT months away!*

*Bob Bryant Hitchin Comet 14 Nov 02*

### *ROBBIE'S TICKET ROUT*

*Robbie Williams has gone one better than Oasis by adding a third date at Knebworth Park after a huge rush on tickets. The singer sold out two planned summer dates in just seven and a half hours when the £35 tickets went on sale at the weekend.* *Daily Express 25 Nov 02*

### *ROBBIE'S TICKET RECORD BREAKER*

*Tickets for the Robbie Williams concerts at Knebworth Park sold out in record-breaking time with more than 1,000 tickets being snapped up PER MINUTE.* *Hertfordshire Mercury 29 Nov 02*

### *ROBBIE'S BIGGEST SINCE THE BEATLES*

*No other singer or band has shifted so many tickets for one venue so quickly. Bands such as Led Zeppelin, Queen and Oasis have been left in Robbie's wake. It makes him without doubt the biggest British pop phenomenon since the Fab Fou*

*The Sun 25 Nov 0*

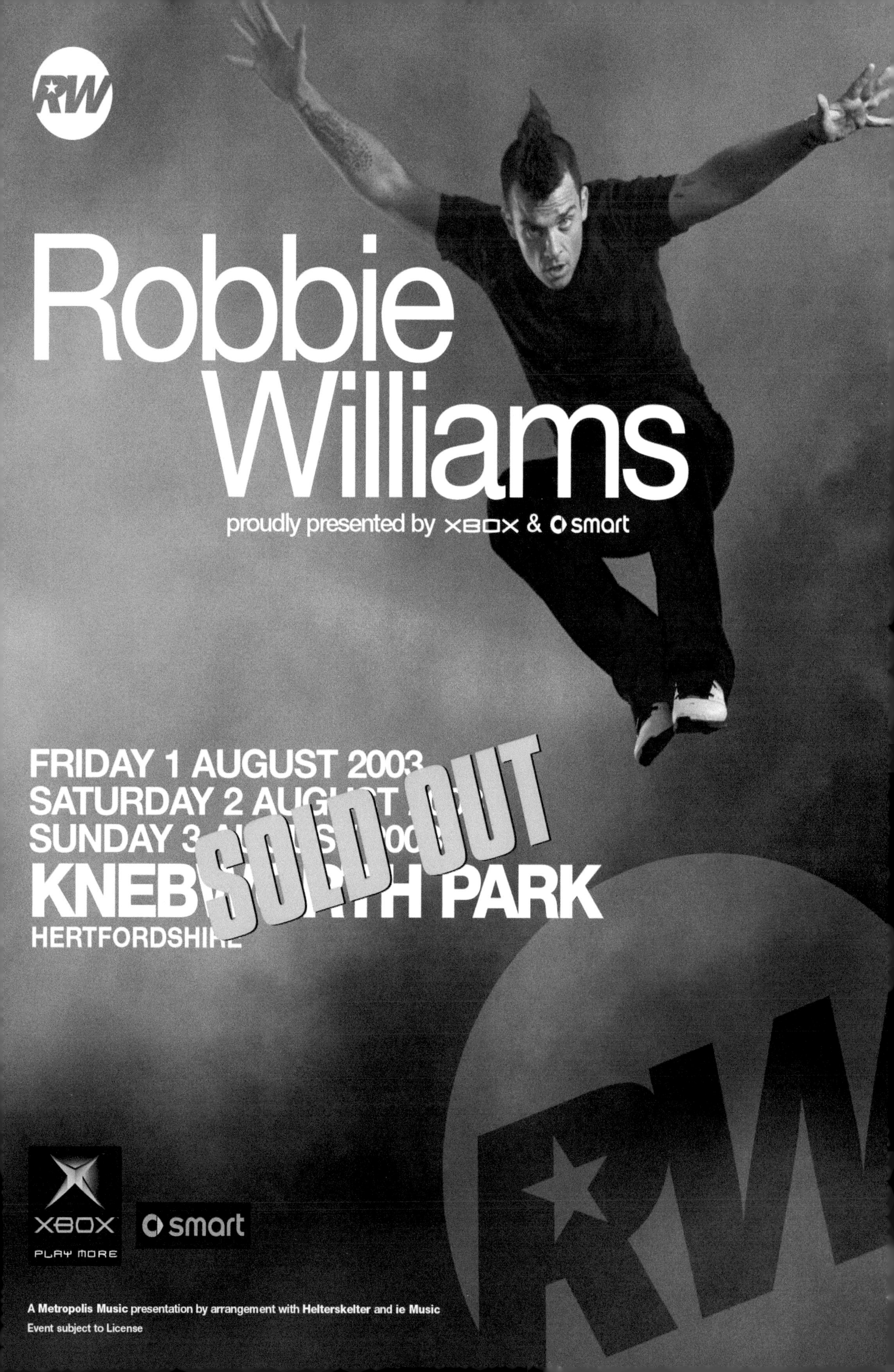
RW
Robbie
Williams
proudly presented by XBOX & smart
FRIDAY 1 AUGUST 2003
SATURDAY 2 AU
SUNDAY 3
KNEB
H PARK
HERTFORDSHI
SOLD OUT
XBOX
PLAY MORE
smart
RW
A Metropolis Music presentation by arrangement with Helterskelter and ie Music
Event subject to License

So who's next?

# KNEBWORTH '74

*Audience recordings of Van Morrison, The Mahavishnu Orchestra and Tim Buckley exist. The poster is available as a reprint from www.rockmusic memorabilia.com.*

# KNEBWORTH '75

*Audience recordings of Steve Miller and Captain Beefheart exist, but this bootleg of Pink Floyd's performance is a little easier to find.*

*A poster reprint is available from www.rockmusicmemorabilia.com*

# KNEBWORTH '76

*Despite some truly wonderful moments - a vintage "Wild Horses" for instance - the Stones have hidden their Michael Lindsay-Hogg directed film of Knebworth '76 so you'll have to make do with the dodgy VHS bootleg or the even dodgier bootleg recordings.*

*The brilliant, circular poster from Knebworth '76 is available as a reprint from www.rockmusic memorabilia.com, or, in limited numbers, as an original from www.knebworthhousegiftshop.com*

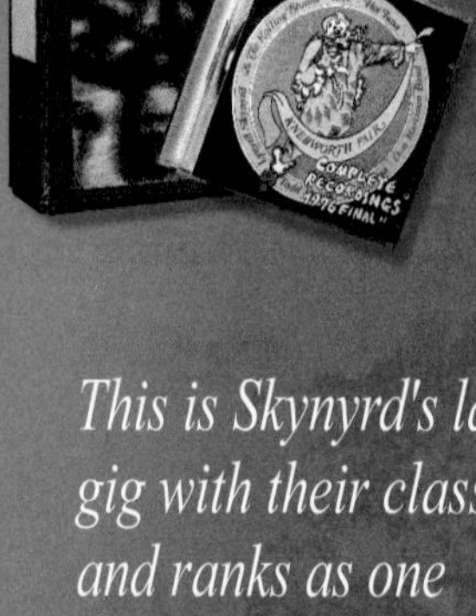


*Alternatively get hold of a copy of "Freebird The Movie" (www.amazon.com) and see why Knebworth '76 is remembered by many as Lynyrd Skynyrd's show.*

*This is Skynyrd's last recorded gig with their classic line-up and ranks as one of the best concert films of all time.*

# ABILIA

## KNEBWORTH '78

*Poster reprints of the two '78 concerts are available from www.rockmusic memorabilia.com*

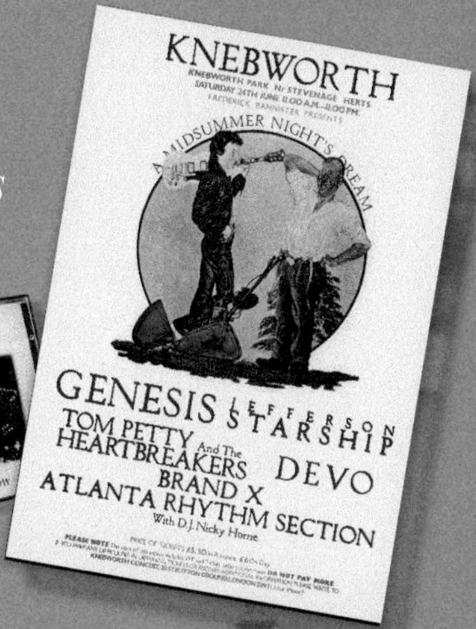


*A Genesis bootleg (right) is rare and an audience recording of Frank Zappa even rarer.*

## KNEBWORTH '79

*At last, some of Zeppelin's last British performance is available on a remastered DVD. Previously you had to make do with multi-generation bootleg VHS or find one of the, albeit nicely packaged, bootleg recordings. A reprint of the poster (not shown) is available from www.rockmusicmemorabilia.com*

*Freddy Bannister's magnificent box set "There Must Be A Better Way" contains reprints of every single ticket, flyer and programme from every single Knebworth concert of the Seventies. It also includes a collection of beautiful stills from every show and a fascinating account of Freddy's Knebworth experiences. Tucked deep in the box is a special bonus, that you'll have to buy it to find! This limited edition is available from www.rockmusicmemorabilia.com*

*See also these two excellent websites: http://tinpan.fortunecity.com/ebony/546/kneb74-program.html & http://www.geocities.com/SunsetStrip/Hotel/8117/Knebworth01.html*

MEMOR

# KNEBWORTH '80

*The Beach Boys' last ever recorded performance by the original line-up used only to be available on an obscure Italian import (left, top) but now has been widely released by Eagle Rock in beautiful remastered CD and DVD versions (left)*

*Mike Oldfield's Knebworth '80 performance is featured in Virgin Video's "The Essential Mike Oldfield", now rare*

# KNEBWORTH '85

*Deep Purple's "In The Absence Of Pink" recording of Knebworth '85 is rare but still available via www.connoisseurcollection.co.uk*

# KNEBWORTH '86

*Queen's last ever concert with Freddie Mercury is available in all manner of bizarre bootlegs including a wobbly video of the concert projection screen, but the official "Live Magic" CD is a better starter and volume three of the documentary "Magic Years" includes wonderful Knebworth footage, including classic aerial views.*

# ABILIA

## KNEBWORTH '90

*To the right of the rare Pink Floyd bootleg are what you used to be able to buy; to the left is the spanking new remastered DVD that you can now buy.*

*Visit the Nordoff Robbins website at http://www.nordoff-robbins.org.uk/*

## KNEBWORTH '96

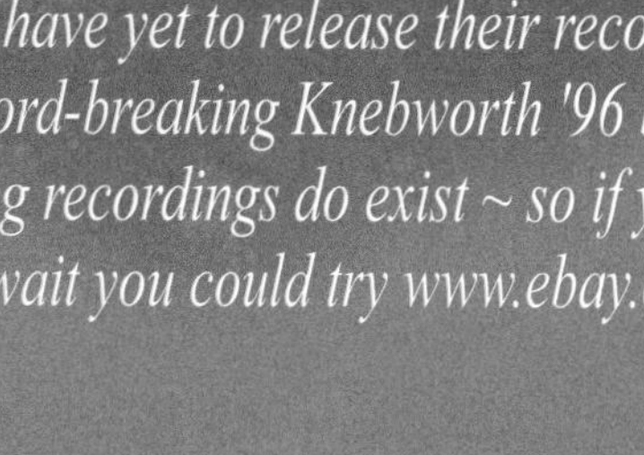


*Oasis have yet to release their recording of record-breaking Knebworth '96 but bootleg recordings do exist ~ so if you can't wait you could try www.ebay.com*

*Chryssie Lytton Cobbold's well-thumbed and much loved book covers the years 1974-1985 but is now hard to find ~ try www.abebooks.com*

*Visit the Knebworth House websites at http://www.knebworthhouse.com & http://www.knebworthhousegiftshop.com*

# ALSO AVAILABLE FROM THE 39...

*"HENRY COBBOLD'S MINI-MASTERPIECE... achieves a double first. It is the first nudist novel (or novella) and the first in graphic form."*

*- H&E -*

*"The comic book artistry is magnificent."*

*- Naturally -*

*"It's like the missing link between Asterix and Milo Manara... Why aren't there more books like this?"*

*- Borderline -*

*"God knows what would have happened if Tintin had got mixed up in all this, but Hergé is evidently an influence... a charming, funny book"*

*- The Erotic Review -*

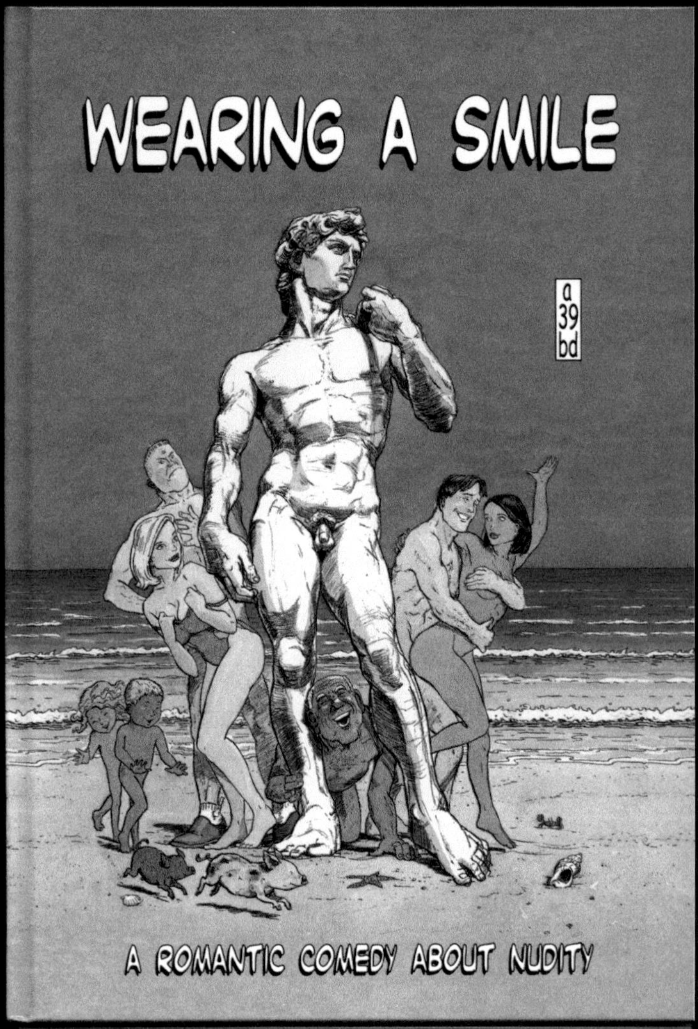

www.wearingasmile.com